Communion of the Sick

THE LITURGICAL PRESS

COLLEGEVILLE   MINNESOTA

The two rites which follow are taken from the ritual book, *Pastoral Care of the Sick: Rite of Anointing and Viaticum,* which represents a careful reworking for English-speaking countries of the first revisions of these rites published after the Second Vatican Council. The numbers which appear to the left of various paragraphs are from the full ritual book, which provides for visits to and anointing of the sick, and for various rites and prayers with those who are dying.

For the convenience of the minister of communion, outlines of the rites appear on pages 10 and 24. The minister should be thoroughly familiar with the introductions (nos. 71–76 and 78–80) and with all the options in the rite.

The English translation, original texts, and arrangement of *Communion of the Sick* (Chapter Three) from *Pastoral Care of the Sick: Rites of Anointing and Viaticum* © 1982, International Committee on English in the Liturgy, Inc. (ICEL). All rights reserved.

Scripture texts used in this work are taken from the *Lectionary for Mass* © 2001, 1998, 1992, 1986, 1970 Confraternity of Christian Doctrine, Washington, D.C. All rights reserved.

General Intercessions and Commentaries on the Readings from Scripture © 1984 by the Order of Saint Benedict, Collegeville, Minnesota 56321.

Published by authority of the Bishops' Committee on the Liturgy, United States Conference of Catholic Bishops.

© 1984, 2003 by the Order of Saint Benedict, Collegeville, Minnesota 56321. All rights reserved. Printed in the United States of America.

ISBN 0-8146-1368-3

CONTENTS

PRAYER OF PREPARATION 4

FOREWORD 5

COMMUNION IN ORDINARY
CIRCUMSTANCES

Introduction 7
Outline of the Rite 10
Introductory Rites 11
Liturgy of the Word .14
Liturgy of Holy Communion 17
Concluding Rite 20

COMMUNION IN A HOSPITAL OR
INSTITUTION

Introduction 23
Outline of the Rite 24
Introductory Rite 25
Liturgy of Holy Communion 26
Concluding Rite 28

APPENDIX

Readings from Sacred Scripture 30
Commentary on the Readings from
    Sacred Scripture 34
General Intercessions 39
Psalms 44

PRAYER OF PREPARATION
FOR THE MINISTER

Almighty God, Father of our Lord Jesus Christ, you are the Father of mercies and the God of all consolation. You comfort us in all our afflictions and thus enable us to comfort those who are in trouble, with the same consolation we receive from you.

God of compassion, fill me with the power of your Word and the love of your Holy Spirit as I visit your suffering sons and daughters. Help me so that I may worthily and gracefully share your sacred presence with those who await your coming to them. May the body and blood of your Son Jesus Christ heal and comfort us, deepen our faith, and strengthen our hope in the imperishable inheritance you have promised to those who seek you.

Father, I pray to you for myself and for those I visit, in the saving name of Jesus, our risen Lord, who lives and reigns with you and the Holy Spirit, now and forever. Amen.

FOREWORD

This service booklet is published in response to requests from ministers of communion, and it is structured and designed primarily for their use. Nevertheless, others who wish to visit and pray with the sick will, we believe, find help here. And many sick or confined persons will benefit from having this book for their private use as well.

Communion of the Sick includes the official instructions, rites, and texts for ordinary "communion calls" to the sick and confined—plus special texts for a sick child—as well as the special rite for communion calls in a hospital or institution. Each has its particular instructions and format, which appear immediately before the rite itself.

Additional features have been added to the official rite with a view to offering ministers some of the help they have requested. These appear in the Appendix beginning on page 30 and include:

1. Additional readings from Sacred Scripture, to provide a wider variety of texts (five passages are included in the rite itself). The Church since Vatican II has desired broad selection of Scripture readings.

2. Brief commentaries in the form of meditations follow. They are lettered A to K, corresponding to the Scripture reading of the same letter. These meditations may be used as they appear, or they may serve as springboards for the visitor's own words.

3. Five sets of General Intercessions appear after the meditations. Again, they may be modified or used as they appear. Creative ministers may choose to select one or two petitions from several sets, as they consider what is most appropriate for the unique person they are visiting. Concern for the larger community should never be overlooked, however.

4. Finally, five psalms have been included at the end of the book. The minister's discretion will determine how one or another psalm may be used—as a prayer to conclude the visit, or perhaps as a preparation for the rite of communion.

Our prayerful hope is that many compassionate members of Christ's body, with or without professional preparation as ministers, will find this little booklet helpful for themselves and for those they visit in the Lord. To him be glory and praise forever.

COMMUNION IN ORDINARY CIRCUMSTANCES

INTRODUCTION

Whoever eats this bread will live for ever.

COMMUNION IN ORDINARY CIRCUMSTANCES

71 This booklet contains two rites: one for use when communion can be celebrated in the context of a liturgy of the word; the other, a brief communion rite for use in more restrictive circumstances, such as in hospitals.

72 Priests with pastoral responsibilities should see to it that the sick or aged, even though not seriously ill or in danger of death, are given every opportunity to receive the eucharist frequently, even daily, especially during the Easter season. They may receive communion at any hour. Those who care for the sick may receive communion with them, in accord with the usual norms. To provide frequent communion for the sick, it may be necessary to ensure that the community has a sufficient number of ministers of communion. The communion minister should wear attire appropriate to this ministry.

The sick person and others may help to plan the celebration, for example, by choosing the prayers and readings. Those making these choices should keep in mind the condition of the sick person. The readings and the homily should help those present to reach a deeper understanding of the mystery of human suffering in relation to the paschal mystery of Christ.

73   The faithful who are ill are deprived of their rightful and accustomed place in the eucharistic community. In bringing communion to them the minister of communion represents Christ and manifests faith and charity on behalf of the whole community toward those who cannot be present at the eucharist. For the sick the reception of communion is not only a privilege but also a sign of support and concern shown by the Christian community for its members who are ill.

The links between the community's eucharistic celebration, especially on the Lord's Day, and the communion of the sick are intimate and manifold. Besides remembering the sick in the general intercessions at Mass, those present should be reminded occasionally of the significance of communion in the lives of those who are ill: union with Christ in his struggle with evil, his prayer for the world, and his love for the Father, and union with the community from which they are separated.

The obligation to visit and comfort those who cannot take part in the eucharistic assembly may be clearly demonstrated by taking communion to them from the community's eucharistic celebration. This symbol of unity between the community and its sick members has the deepest significance on the Lord's Day, the special day of the eucharistic assembly.

74 When the eucharist is brought to the sick, it should be carried in a pyx or small closed container. Those who are with the sick should be asked to prepare a table covered with a linen cloth upon which the blessed sacrament will be placed. Lighted candles are prepared and, where it is customary, a vessel of holy water. Care should be taken to make the occasion special and joyful.

Sick people who are unable to receive communion under the form of bread may receive it under the form of wine alone. If the wine is consecrated at a Mass not celebrated in the presence of the sick person, the blood of the Lord is kept in a properly covered vessel and is placed in the tabernacle after communion. The precious blood should be carried to the sick in a vessel which is closed in such a way as to eliminate all danger of spilling. If some of the precious blood remains, it should be consumed by the minister, who should also see to it that the vessel is properly purified.

75 If the sick wish to celebrate the sacrament of penance, it is preferable that the priest make himself available for this during a previous visit.

76 If it is necessary to celebrate the sacrament of penance during the rite of communion, it takes the place of the penitential rite.

OUTLINE OF THE RITE

INTRODUCTORY RITES
Greeting
Sprinkling with Holy Water
Penitential Rite

LITURGY OF THE WORD
Reading
Response
General Intercessions

LITURGY OF HOLY COMMUNION
The Lord's Prayer
Communion
Silent Prayer
Prayer after Communion

CONCLUDING RITE
Blessing

INTRODUCTORY RITES

GREETING

81 The minister greets the sick person and the others present. One of the following may be used:

A Minister: The peace of the Lord be with you always.

All: And also with you.

B Minister: Peace be with you (this house) and with all who live here.

All: And also with you.

C Minister: The grace of our Lord Jesus Christ and the love of God and the fellowship of the Holy Spirit be with you all.

All: And also with you.

D Minister: The grace and peace of God our Father and the Lord Jesus Christ be with you.

All: And also with you.

The minister then places the blessed sacrament on the table, and all join in adoration.

SPRINKLING WITH HOLY WATER

82   If it seems desirable, the priest or deacon may sprinkle the sick person and those present with holy water. One of the following may be used.:

A   Let this water call to mind our baptism into Christ, who by his death and resurrection has redeemed us.

B   Like a stream in parched land,
may the grace of the Lord
refresh our lives.

If the sacrament of penance is now celebrated, the penitential rite is omitted.

PENITENTIAL RITE

83   The minister invites the sick person and all present to join in the penitential rite, using these or similar words:

A   My brothers and sisters, to prepare ourselves for this celebration, let us call to mind our sins.

B   My brothers and sisters, let us turn with confidence to the Lord and ask his forgiveness for all our sins.

After a brief period of silence, the penitential rite continues, using one of the following:

A Minister: Lord Jesus, you healed the sick:
Lord, have mercy.

   All: Lord, have mercy.

   Minister: Lord Jesus, you forgave sinners:
Christ, have mercy.

   All: Christ, have mercy.

   Minister: Lord Jesus, you give us
yourself to heal us
and bring us strength:
Lord, have mercy.

   All: Lord, have mercy.

B All say:

I confess to almighty God,
and to you, my brothers and sisters,
that I have sinned through my own fault

They strike their breast.

in my thoughts and in my words,
in what I have done,
and in what I have failed to do;
and I ask blessed Mary, ever virgin,
all the angels and saints,
and you, my brothers and sisters,
to pray for me to the Lord our God.

The minister concludes the penitential rite with the following:

> May almighty God have mercy on us,
> forgive us our sins,
> and bring us to everlasting life.

All: Amen.

LITURGY OF THE WORD

READING

84   The word of God is proclaimed by one of those present or by the minister. In place of the following readings, the minister may choose a reading from among those on pages 30–33 of this book, or one from Part III of *Pastoral Care of the Sick: Rites of Anointing and Viaticum.*

A   John 6:51

> A reading from the holy Gospel
> according to John

> Jesus says: "I am the living bread that came down from heaven; whoever eats this bread will live forever; and the bread that I will give is my Flesh for the life of the world."

> The Gospel of the Lord.

For commentary see A on page 34.

B John 6:54-58

A reading from the holy Gospel
according to John

Jesus says: "Whoever eats my Flesh and drinks my Blood has eternal life, and I will raise him on the last day. For my Flesh is true food, and my Blood is true drink. Whoever eats my Flesh and drinks my Blood remains in me and I in him. Just as the living Father sent me and I have life because of the Father, so also the one who feeds on me will have life because of me. This is the bread that came down from heaven. Unlike your ancestors who ate and still died, whoever eats this bread will live forever."

The Gospel of the Lord.

For commentary see B on page 34.

C John 14:6

A reading from the holy Gospel
according to John

Jesus says: "I am the way and the truth and the life. No one comes to the Father except through me.

The Gospel of the Lord.

For commentary see C on page 35.

D John 15:5

> A reading from the holy Gospel
> according to John

Jesus says: "I am the vine, you are the branches. Whoever remains in me and I in him will bear much fruit, because without me you can do nothing."

> The Gospel of the Lord.

For commentary see D on page 35.

E 1 John 4:16

> A reading from the first Letter
> of Saint John

We have come to know and to believe in the love God has for us.

God is love, and whoever remains in love remains in God and God in him.

> The word of the Lord.

For commentary see E on page 36.

Response

85   A brief period of silence may be observed after the reading of the word of God.

The minister may then give a brief explanation of the reading, applying it to the needs of the sick person and those who are looking after him or her. (*See pages 34–38.*)

General Intercessions

86   The general intercessions may be said. With a brief introduction the minister invites all those present to pray. After the intentions the minister says the concluding prayer. It is desirable that the intentions be announced by someone other than the minister. (*See pages 39–43.*)

LITURGY OF HOLY COMMUNION

The Lord's Prayer

87   The minister introduces the Lord's Prayer in these or similar words:

A   Now let us pray as Christ the Lord has taught us:

B   And now let us pray with confidence as Christ our Lord commanded:

All say:

Our Father . . .

COMMUNION

88 The minister shows the eucharistic bread to those present, saying:

A This is the bread of life.
Taste and see that the Lord is good.

B This is the Lamb of God
who takes away the sins of the world.
Happy are those who are called to his supper.

The sick person and all who are to receive communion say:

Lord, I am not worthy to receive you,
but only say the word and I shall be healed.

The minister goes to the sick person and, showing the blessed sacrament, says:

The body of Christ.
(and/or The blood of Christ.)

The sick person answers: **Amen**, and receives communion.

Others present who wish to receive communion then do so in the usual way.

After the conclusion of the rite, the minister cleanses the vessel as usual.

SILENT PRAYER

89   Then a period of silence may be observed.

PRAYER AFTER COMMUNION

90   The minister says a concluding prayer. One of the following may be used:

Let us pray.

Pause for silent prayer, if this has not preceded.

A   God our Father,
you have called us to share the one bread
    and one cup
and so become one in Christ.
Help us to live in him
that we may bear fruit,
rejoicing that he has redeemed the world.
We ask this through Christ our Lord.
All: Amen.

B   All-powerful God,
we thank you for the nourishment you give us
through your holy gift.
Pour out your Spirit upon us
and in the strength of this food from heaven
keep us single-minded in your service.
We ask this in the name of Jesus the Lord.
All: Amen.

C   All-powerful and ever-living God,
    may the body and blood of Christ your Son
    be for our brother/sister N.
    a lasting remedy for body and soul.
    We ask this through Christ our Lord.
    All: Amen.

CONCLUDING RITE

Blessing

91   The priest or deacon blesses the sick person and the
others present, using one of the following blessings. If,
however, any of the blessed sacrament remains, he may bless
the sick person by making a sign of the cross with the blessed
sacrament, in silence.

A   Priest: May God the Father bless you.
    All: Amen.

    Priest: May God the Son heal you.
    All: Amen.

    Priest: May God the Holy Spirit enlighten
              you.
    All: Amen.

    Priest: May almighty God bless you,
              the Father, and the Son, ✝ and the
              Holy Spirit.
    All: Amen.

B   Priest: May the Lord be with you to
              protect you.
    All: Amen.

Priest: May he guide you and give you
        strength.

All: Amen.

Priest: May he watch over you, keep you in
        his care, and bless you with his
        peace.

All: Amen.

Priest: May almighty God bless you,
the Father, and the Son, ✝ and the
        Holy Spirit.

All: Amen.

C Priest: May the blessing of almighty God,
the Father, and the Son, ✝ and the
        Holy Spirit,
come upon you and remain with
        you for ever.

All: Amen.

A minister who is not a priest or deacon invokes God's
blessing and makes the sign of the cross on himself or herself,
while saying:

A Minister: May the Lord bless us,
protect us from all evil,
and bring us to everlasting life.

All: Amen.

B Minister: May the almighty and merciful
        God bless and protect us,
the Father, and the Son, and the
        Holy Spirit.

All: Amen.

COMMUNION IN A HOSPITAL OR INSTITUTION

INTRODUCTION

78   There will be situations, particularly in large institutions with many communicants, when the minister should consider alternative means so that the rite of communion of the sick is not diminished to the absolute minimum. In such cases the following alternatives should be considered: (a) where possible, the residents or patients may be gathered in groups in one or more areas; (b) additional ministers of communion may assist.

When it is not possible to celebrate the full rite, the rite for communion in a hospital or institution may be used. If it is convenient, however, the minister may add elements from the rite for ordinary circumstances, for example, a Scripture reading.

79   The rite begins with the recitation of the eucharistic antiphon in the church, the hospital chapel, or the first room visited. Then the minister gives communion to the sick in their individual rooms.

80   The concluding prayer may be said in the church, the hospital chapel, or the last room visited. No blessing is given.

OUTLINE OF THE RITE

INTRODUCTORY RITE
  Antiphon

LITURGY OF HOLY COMMUNION
  Greeting
  The Lord's Prayer
  Communion

CONCLUDING RITE
  Concluding Prayer

INTRODUCTORY RITE

ANTIPHON

92 The rite may begin in the church, the hospital chapel, or the first room, where the minister says one of the following antiphons:

A How holy this feast
in which Christ is our food:
his passion is recalled;
grace fills our hearts;
and we receive a pledge of the glory to come.

B How gracious are you, Lord:
your gift of bread from heaven
reveals a Father's love and brings us perfect
joy.
You fill the hungry with good things
and send the rich away empty.

C I am the living bread
come down from heaven.
If you eat this bread
you will live for ever.
The bread I will give is my flesh
for the life of the world.

If it is customary, the minister may be accompanied by a person carrying a candle.

LITURGY OF HOLY COMMUNION

GREETING

93   On entering each room, the minister may use one of the following greetings:

A   Minister: The peace of the Lord be with you always.

   All: And also with you.

B   Minister: The grace of our Lord Jesus Christ and the love of God and the fellowship of the Holy Spirit be with you all.

   All: And also with you.

The minister then places the blessed sacrament on the table, and all join in adoration.

If there is time and it seems desirable, the minister may proclaim a Scripture reading from those found on pages 14–16; 30–33 of this book, or those appearing in Part III of *Pastoral Care of the Sick: Rites of Anointing and Viaticum.*

THE LORD'S PRAYER

94   When circumstances permit (for example, when there are not many rooms to visit), the minister is encouraged to lead the sick in the Lord's Prayer. The minister introduces the Lord's Prayer in these or similar words:

A Jesus taught us to call God our Father, and
so we have the courage to say:

B Now let us pray as Christ the Lord has taught
us:

All say:

Our Father . . .

COMMUNION

95 The minister shows the eucharistic bread to those present, saying:

A This is the Lamb of God
who takes away the sins of the world.
Happy are those who hunger and thirst,
for they shall be satisfied.

B This is the bread of life.
Taste and see that the Lord is good.

The sick person and all who are to receive communion say:

Lord, I am not worthy to receive you,
but only say the word and I shall be healed.

The minister goes to the sick person and, showing the blessed sacrament, says:

The body of Christ.
(and/or The blood of Christ.)

The sick person answers: Amen, and receives communion.

Others present who wish to receive communion then do so in the usual way.

CONCLUDING RITE

Concluding Prayer

96   The concluding prayer may be said either in the last room visited, in the church, or chapel. One of the following may be used.

Let us pray.

Pause for silent prayer.

A   God our Father,
       you have called us to share the one bread
           and one cup
       and so become one in Christ.
       Help us to live in him
       that we may bear fruit,
       rejoicing that he has redeemed the world.
       We ask this through Christ our Lord.
       All: Amen.

B   All-powerful and ever-living God,
       may the body and blood of Christ your Son
       be for our brothers and sisters
       a lasting remedy for body and soul.
       We ask this through Christ our Lord.
       All: Amen.

C All-powerful God,
   we thank you for the nourishment you give us
   through your holy gift.
   Pour out your Spirit upon us
   and in the strength of this food from heaven
   keep us single-minded in your service.
   We ask this in the name of Jesus the Lord.
   All: Amen.

The blessing is omitted and the minister cleanses the vessel as usual.

APPENDIX

READINGS FROM SACRED SCRIPTURE

The following readings may be used in place of those given on pages 14–16. They are taken from Part III of *Pastoral Care of the Sick: Rites of Anointing and Viaticum.*

F Romans 8:26-27

A reading from the Letter of Saint Paul to the Romans

In the same way, the Spirit too comes to the aid of our weakness; for we do not know how to pray as we ought, but the Spirit himself intercedes with inexpressible groanings. And the one who searches hearts knows what is the intention of the Spirit, because it intercedes for the holy ones according to God's will.

The word of the Lord.

For commentary see F on page 36.

G Romans 8:31b-35, 37-39

A reading from the Letter of Saint Paul to the Romans

Brothers and sisters: If God is for us, who can be against us? He who did not spare his own Son but handed him over for us all, how will he not also give us everything else along with him? Who will bring a charge against God's chosen ones? It is God who acquits us. Who will condemn? It is Christ Jesus who died, rather, was raised, who also is at the right hand of God, who indeed interecedes for us. What will separate us from the love of Christ? Will anguish, or distress or persecution, or famine, or nakedness, or peril, or the sword?

No, in all these things, we conquer overwhelmingly through him who loved us. For I am convinced that neither death, nor life, nor angels, nor principalities, nor present things, nor future things, nor powers, nor height, nor depth, nor any other creature will be able to separate us from the love of God in Christ Jesus our Lord.

The word of the Lord.

For commentary see G on page 37.

H 1 Corinthians 15:1-4

A reading from the first Letter of
Saint Paul to the Corinthians

I am reminding you, brothers and sisters, of the Gospel I preached to you, which you indeed received and in which you also stand. Through it you are also being saved, if you hold fast to the word I preached to you, unless you believed in vain. For I handed on to you as of first importance what I also received: that Christ died for our sins in accordance with the Scriptures; that he was buried; that he was raised on the third day in accordance with the Scriptures.

The word of the Lord.

For commentary see H on page 37.

I 2 Corinthians 4:16-18

A reading from the second Letter of Saint Paul to the Corinthians

Brothers and sisters: We are not discouraged; rather, although our outer self is wasting away, our inner self is being renewed day by day. For this momentary light affliction is producing for us an eternal weight of glory beyond all comparison, as we look not to what is seen but to what is unseen; for what is seen is transitory, but what is unseen is eternal.

The word of the Lord.

For commentary see I on page 38.

Especially for visits to children from chapter II of *Pastoral Care of the Sick: Rites of Anointing and Viaticum.*

J Mark 9:33-37

A reading from the holy Gospel according to Mark

Jesus and his disciples came to Capernaum and, once inside the house, he began to ask them, "What were you arguing about on the way?" But they remained silent. They had been discussing among themselves who was the greatest. Then he sat down, called the Twelve, and said to them, "If anyone wishes to be first, he shall be the last of all and the servant of all." Taking a child he placed it in their midst, and putting his arms around it he said to them, "Whoever receives one child such as this in my name, receives me; and whoever receives me, receives not me but the One who sent me."

The Gospel of the Lord.

For commentary see J and K on page 38.

K Mark 10:13-16

A reading from the holy Gospel
according to Mark

People were bringing children to Jesus that he might touch them, but the disciples rebuked them. When Jesus saw this he became indignant and said to them, "Let the children come to me; do not prevent them, for the Kingdom of God belongs to such as these. Amen, I say to you, whoever does not accept the Kingdom of God like a child will not enter it." Then he embraced them and blessed them, placing his hands on them.

The Gospel of the Lord.

For commentary see J and K on page 38.

COMMENTARY ON THE READINGS
FROM SACRED SCRIPTURE

These commentaries correspond to Scripture readings A–E given in the rite (*pages 14–16*) and readings F–K in the Appendix (*pages 30–33*). (*See No. 85, page 17*).

A John 6:51

Jesus tells us that he wants to stay close to us. In fact, he assures us that in the Eucharist the bread and wine become his body and blood for the life of the world. Christ's life is his gift to us. His love is his gift to us. His constant, strengthening, and comforting company is his gift to us. We find peace in this presence of Jesus, who promises us life now and for eternity. Glory and praise to God, through Jesus Christ our Lord.

B John 6:54-58

Jesus absolutely does not want to let go of us. He looks for all sorts of ways to convince us that he loves us so much that he wants to enjoy our company for all eternity. Jesus feeds us with his own body and blood, spiritual food that brings the very life and love of God into our hearts. Jesus promises that when we receive him in Communion, he lives in us and we live in him. Thanks be to God, who holds us forever in his heart.

C John 14:6

How can we go wrong when we give ourselves over to the care of Jesus? The Lord who lived and died and rose to life again tells us that he is leading us step by step to the Father. The body and blood of Jesus heal us, pardon our sins, and give us nourishment on the way. Jesus assures us that we will live forever with God, and our joy will be complete. Glory and praise to our Lord Jesus Christ, who leads us carefully to our Father.

D John 15:5

It is hard to imagine anything more closely connected than a branch and its trunk. Baptism grafts us into Jesus Christ, and we draw our life from his life. Even our weakness is turned into strength by the miracle of God's life in us, and the Eucharist keeps strengthening our union with the Lord. We live in Jesus and Jesus lives in us, helping us to produce good fruit—love, patience, repentance, thankfulness, peace of mind and soul. Yes, Jesus is the vine, and we are his branches, receiving life from him. Blessed be the name of Jesus.

E   John 4:16

How fortunate we are to have the gift of faith! In faith we come to know how much God loves us, and this love of God continually renews and refreshes us. Holy Communion is a grace-giving sign of God's constant, faithful love. God's love is so powerful that it removes our sins, helps us bear suffering along with Christ, and overcomes death, so that we will be raised up in glory to live forever with God. Blessed be God who loves us so much, both now and forever.

F   Romans 8:26-27

Sometimes during sickness people find it particularly hard to pray. They are tired or weak, perhaps, and their concentration wavers. Frustration and sadness can move in. But God's Word tells us not to worry. The Holy Spirit prays in us—in a way we do not understand, but God the Father understands perfectly. So we can accept our weakened condition in peace and simply let the Holy Spirit express our hope, our love, and our most important needs. Thanks be to God, who listens to the Holy Spirit praying for us and in us. We have God's Word on this.

G Romans 8:31b-35, 37-39

Physical suffering and weakness can play tricks on our mind. We think of many problems but can't do anything to resolve them. Sometimes the memory of past sins brings sadness or even fear of losing God's love. But God tells us not to worry—nothing can separate us from the love of Christ, who died for our sins, washing them away in the blood of the cross. Neither sickness nor death can take away God's love. Nothing can stop Jesus from loving us, forgiving us, and embracing us joyfully forever. To God, who loves us so much when we are tired and weak, be glory and praise forever.

H 1 Corinthians 15:1-4

Sometimes it seems that God is so far away, even unconcerned. Jesus felt that way on the cross, but he still trusted his Father. Jesus told his Father that he felt abandoned, but then he prayed in hope: "Father, I put my life in your hands." The Father was with Jesus in his death on the cross and raised him to life in glory. Whatever our trouble, God assures us that he is with us through it all. Holy Communion seals God's promise and brings him to you right now. Because God is faithful and true, we can pray: "Father, I put my life in your hands," through Jesus Christ our Lord.

I   2 Corinthians 4:16-18

It is hard to believe that suffering and weakness can be very strong medicine. Since Jesus suffered willingly for our sake, the cross of suffering will always be a sign of God's saving love for us. When we unite our sufferings to the cross of Jesus, we experience a spiritual power beyond human understanding. In union with Jesus, our cross leads us to new life, for ourselves and for others. The Eucharist recalls the powerful dying and rising of Jesus. It deepens our union with Jesus and becomes strong medicine to heal us. Glory and praise to Jesus our Lord.

J and K   Mark 9:33-37 *and* Mark 10:13-16

Jesus loves children very much. From children we can learn how to trust God and how to be open to God's gift of health and life. Jesus protects children, hugs them and blesses them, cures them and restores them to their parents. Yes, Jesus loves and cares for children more than we can say. Praise and thanks to Jesus for his gentle, loving care.

GENERAL INTERCESSIONS

The general intercessions may be said after the commentary on the reading from Sacred Scripture (*pages 34–38*). The minister invites all those present to pray. *(See No. 86).* A selection of any of the following may be used or any others chosen by the minister or those present.

1

Minister: Mindful of other people's needs as well as our own, let us pray.

1. For stronger belief in the promises of Jesus, we pray:

   All: Lord, hear our prayer.

2. For people who do not believe in God's presence, we pray:

   All: Lord, hear our prayer.

3. For people who have grown bitter from their suffering, we pray:

   All: Lord, hear our prayer.

4. For people afraid of what the future will bring, we pray:

   All: Lord, hear our prayer.

5. For hearts always grateful for the gift of Jesus in Holy Communion, we pray:

   All: Lord, hear our prayer.

Minister: Lord God, we believe that your love is always giving us life and hope. We believe that you are here with us now. We pray through Christ our Lord.

   All: Amen.

2

Minister: Let us turn to God, from whom all good gifts come, and pray for all our brothers and sisters.

1. For the Church and all who minister to people in need, we pray:
   All: Lord, hear us.

2. For those who do not know God's love in their lives, we pray:
   All: Lord, hear us.

3. For people troubled by painful memories and fears, we pray:
   All: Lord, hear us.

4. For people who are sick or lonely, we pray:
   All: Lord, hear us.

5. For stronger hope in God, the source of our joy, we pray:
   All: Lord, hear us.

Minister: Lord God, moved by your Holy Spirit we ask you to pour out upon your people, and especially upon N., the gifts you know are most important right now. Through Christ our Lord.
   All: Amen.

3

Minister: God asks us to turn to him in our
           need, and so we pray for ourselves
           and for all who are in need.

1. That God may pour healing grace into all who
   are sick, we pray:
       All: Lord, hear our prayer.

2. That God may raise the hopes of all who suf-
   fer anxiety, we pray:
       All: Lord, hear our prayer.

3. That God may give strength to all who care
   for the sick, we pray:
       All: Lord, hear our prayer.

4. That God may comfort those who sorrow and
   mourn, we pray:
       All: Lord, hear our prayer.

5. That God may give peace and joy to those who
   seek him, we pray:
       All: Lord, hear our prayer.

Minister: Loving Lord, God of mercy, we
           believe you are quick to hear us as we
           call to you. Bless us with the gifts and
           graces that you know are best for us.
           We pray in the name of Jesus, our
           Lord now and forever.
       All: Amen.

4

Minister: In prayer now let us remember all God's people and ask the Lord for his loving mercy.

1. For peace and harmony among all nations and peoples, we pray:
   All: Lord, have mercy.

2. For the forgiveness of our sins and the grace to be faithful, we pray:
   All: Lord, have mercy.

3. For the healing of hurts and resentments, and the grace to forgive others, we pray:
   All: Lord, have mercy.

4. For health and wholeness in body, mind, and spirit, we pray:
   All: Lord, have mercy.

5. For the comfort and joy of God's presence in us, we pray:
   All: Lord, have mercy.

Minister: Lord God, you are the Father of mercies. In Jesus you have reconciled everyone to yourself. Your Holy Spirit continually breathes new life into us. We praise and thank you in the name of Jesus, who unites us to you both now and forever.
   All: Amen.

FOR A SICK CHILD

Minister: Let us pray now, asking God to help and to heal N. and all who are suffering.

1. May God bless N. in this time of sickness, we pray:
    All: Lord, hear our prayer.

2. May God comfort N.'s family and give them peace, we pray:
    All: Lord, hear our prayer.

3. May God help us to trust in his healing power, we pray:
    All: Lord, hear our prayer.

4. May God guide all doctors and nurses in their work of healing, we pray:
    All: Lord, hear our prayer.

5. May God heal all who are sick in body, mind, or spirit, we pray:
    All: Lord, hear our prayer.

Minister: Lord Jesus, we trust in your power to heal and to save, for you are Lord of life both now and forever.
    All: Amen.

Psalm 23:1-6

The LORD is my shepherd; I shall not want.
    In verdant pastures he gives me repose;
Beside restful waters he leads me;
    he refreshes my soul.

He guides in right paths
    for his name's sake.
Even though I walk in the dark valley
    I fear no evil; for you are at my side
With your rod and your staff
    that give me courage.

You spread the table before me
    in the sight of my foes;
You anoint my head with oil;
    my cup overflows.

Only goodness and kindness follow me
    all the days of my life;
And I shall dwell in the house of the LORD
    for years to come.

Psalm 34:1–9

I will bless the LORD at all times;
  his praise shall be ever in my mouth.
Let my soul glory in the LORD;
  the lowly will hear me and be glad.

Glorify the LORD with me,
  let us together extol his name.
I sought the LORD, and he answered me
  and delivered me from all my fears.

Look to him that you may be radiant
    with joy,
  and your faces may not blush with
    shame.
When the afflicted man called out,
    the LORD heard,
  and from all his distress he saved him.
The angel of the LORD encamps
  around those who fear him, and delivers
    them.
Taste and see how good the LORD is;
  happy the man who takes refuge in him.

Psalm 63:1-9

O God, you are my God whom I seek;
  for you my flesh pines and my soul
    thirsts
  like the earth, parched, lifeless and
    without water.
Thus have I gazed toward you in the
    sanctuary
  to see your power and your glory.

For your kindness is a greater good than
    life;
  my lips shall glorify you.
Thus will I bless you while I live;
  lifting up my hands, I will call upon
    your name.
As with the riches of a banquet shall my
    soul be satisfied,
  and with exultant lips my mouth shall
    praise you.

I will remember you upon my couch,
  and through the night-watches I will
    meditate on you:
That you are my help,
  and in the shadow of your wings I shout
    for joy.

My soul clings fast to you;
  your right hand upholds me.

Psalm 84:1-4, 9-12

How lovely is your dwelling place,
  O LORD of hosts!
My soul yearns and pines
  for the courts of the LORD.
My heart and my flesh
  cry out for the living God.

Even the sparrow finds a home,
  and the swallow a nest
  in which she puts her young—
Your altars, O LORD of hosts,
  my king and my God!

O LORD of hosts, hear my prayer;
  hearken, O God of Jacob!
O God, behold our shield,
  and look upon the face of your anointed.

I had rather one day in your courts
  than a thousand elsewhere;
I had rather lie at the threshold of the
    house of my God
  than dwell in the tents of the wicked.

For a sun and a shield is the LORD God;
  grace and glory he bestows;
The LORD withholds no good thing
  from those who walk in sincerity.

Psalm 103:1-6, 8, 10-13

Bless the LORD, O my soul;
  and all my being, bless his holy name.
Bless the LORD, O my soul,
  and forget not all his benefits;
He pardons all your iniquities,
  he heals all your ills.
He redeems your life from destruction,
  he crowns you with kindness and
    compassion,
He fills your lifetime with good;
  your youth is renewed like the eagle's.

The LORD secures justice
  and the rights of all the oppressed.
Merciful and gracious is the LORD,
  slow to anger and abounding in kindness.
Not according to our sins does he deal with
    us,
  nor does he requite us according to our
    crimes.

For as the heavens are high above the
    earth,
  so surpassing is his kindness toward those
    who fear him.
As far as the east is from the west,
  so far has he put our transgressions from
    us.
As a father has compassion on his children,
  so the LORD has compassion on those
    who fear him.